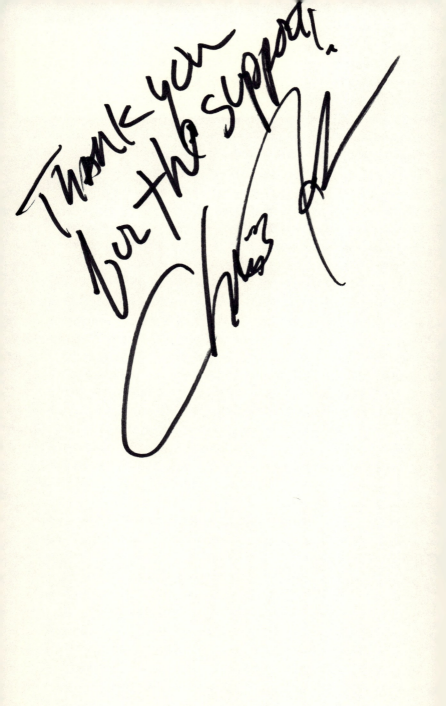

Getting Dressed From The Inside

by

Christopher Johnson

authorHOUSE®

AuthorHouse™
1663 Liberty Drive, Suite 200
Bloomington, IN 47403
www.authorhouse.com
Phone: 1-800-839-8640

*Scriptures noted NKJV are taken from the
New King James Version Bible*

*Scriptures noted AMP are taken from scripture quotations
taken from The Amplified Bible, copyright 1954,1958,
1962,1964, 1965, 1987, by Lockman Foundation.*

First published by AuthorHouse 11/29/2007
ISBN: 978-1-4343-5399-3 (sc)
Library of Congress Control Number: 2007909176

Printed in the United States of America
Bloomington, Indiana

This book is printed on acid-free paper.

I would like to dedicate this book to my little girl "SJ". I am so sad I never got the chance to hold you in my arms. But rest assured, Daddy is down here trying to make this world a better place. I can't wait until the day I get to see you in Heaven!

This book is in memory of my grandmother "nanny" I miss you and I wish you were here so I could read my first book to you! My cousin Claude "aka Mark" I love you man thanks for looking out for me up there in Heaven! Tell Ebony I said what's up! To my step mom Mary Nixon I wish you were here to celebrate with me I miss watching your dance moves (funky chicken right)!

And to my son little Christopher, yes daddy is still reading and writing I have not taken a break yet! To my Mom, we did it!

Lord, thank you for allowing me to use my gift to help others realize their full potential. I pray that I have done my best to relay the message and that they may receive it with the best of their ability! Thank You God for your guidance and I can not wait to meet you one day! Amen!

Contents

Preface

GETTING DRESSED FROM The Inside will change your mind instantly on how you approach putting on clothes in your daily routine! I wanted to address how so many of us although draped in name brand clothing can still be so miserable on the inside. I know several people that with the addition of a Versace shirt they can get over what ever they were dealing with once that fabric hits their skin! This is not always the best decision! Your outfit cannot talk for you.

I am not going to hit you like most motivational or inspirational authors do. You know how they start their books off saying; *"If I met you today I need only 3mins to tell you what's wrong with you, blah, blah, blah!"* I don't need 3 minutes to tell you, heck I don't even need to meet you to tell you that you think differently about yourself on the inside and out than others do. We all feel a certain way about ourselves. How do I know this? Because we all have secrets or things we don't discuss with anyone. You know the saying; *"No one will ever know about this, I am going to take this to my grave!"* Well I am here to tell you that all the stuff we keep locked away in a safe place inside of us, can damage our outer appearance! Even if nobody knows what it is. This book will help us deal with all of these issues! From how you know that your birth mark is not pretty to how you never want anyone to know you have a perspiration problem. *Getting Dressed From The Inside* will help you understand that what you have on the outside does not matter when your inside is the focal point!

Christopher Johnson has found away for you to deal with whatever inside garbage you are storing up that affects how you feel about yourself! I help you get rid of it! Filled with hilarious anecdotes and true life experiences; and exercises that help you solve the mystery that is you and build upon a new understanding and love for yourself that will change the way you feel about yourself forever!

This pocket size book although small in stature will help you change the big picture, which is how you see yourself! Minor adjustments can help you change your life in a Major way! This book without question is a makeover from the inside out!

Introduction

HAVE YOU EVER had a conversation like this before? "How much time do you need?" "Oh give me about an hour!" "Ok honey I will be down stairs waiting!" "Hmmm it's 7 o' clock and I made the dinner reservations for 8:30. If she is ready at 8 we will have 30 minutes to get there! Great right on time! "Honey are you ok?" "Yes, I am fine, but I can't find my black pumps, my other diamond earring, and the blow dryer keeps over heating!" Ok sweetie how much more time do you need?" "About 15 more minutes." "Ok!" If she can get down here by 8:15 I can take the back streets and we can be there by 8:35. "Honey, are you ok it's 8:20!" "I'm almost ready!" "I can't find the black belt that goes with this black purse!" "Babe, we are going to miss our dinner reservations!" "I'm coming down right now." "I can put my makeup on in the car!" "WHAT!" "You don't even have your makeup on yet!!!"

"When ever we get ready to go out we're never on time because she takes forever to get dressed!

Does this sound familiar? Maybe the conversation you had was with a parent or friend instead of a husband or wife. And maybe you were the one being waited on. Well, I've had this conversation many times! I've spent a lot of time over the years waiting for my mother and other people in my life to get dressed. And I have noticed, during all this waiting, that we spend a large amount of time getting dressed! For work, dinner, church and even dates. We spend countless hours in front of the mirror, in the closet, looking for that matching sock, or looking for the other shoe. By the time you leave this great earth the average person could have easily spent 6 years getting dressed! Think about it, for a moment. Add up the average time it takes you to get ready each day. Now multiply that by 365. You will be surprised when you see how much time you spend putting on clothes or makeup in one year. Numbers may vary depending on how good you want to look (I am just joking)!

When we look at how much time we spend putting on clothes and preparing our exteriors each day, I wonder how much time do we spend preparing our interior to face the day? When I say face the day you may ask, "What do you mean Christopher?" Well, I am happy you asked! I am referring to the way you prepare yourself to handle the negative and positive interactions that make up the 24hrs you are stepping into. Whether at work, at home, or wherever you go, you will deal with external situations that will affect you internally. We know you've spent serious time on your external outfit. How much time have you spent on your internal "infit"? What is your "infit" you may ask? Well, I am happy you asked! Let's start with looking at a typical outfit. Most of us start with our underwear, then shirt, blouse, dress, skirt or pants. Then you may have accessories, gentleman do not trip, you have them too-- hosiery, belt, shoes, watch, earrings, rings, ties, hat and sunglasses! Wow that is a lot when you break it down. Your internal "infit" is more complex. You have your feelings or emotions, confidence, self–esteem, morals, memories, your future goals and plans. I am not going to get too philosophical, but you have more thoughts per day then there are cars on the road from California to New York! However, you can only wear one outfit at a time (unless you live some place really cold). Internally you can have on 7 different "infit's" at the same time.

Have you ever had a moment where you were elated about something, and immediately some guy cuts you off in traffic; your favorite song comes on the radio; then your best friend calls to tell you good news. In the span of 2 minutes you have changed your inner "infit" 4 times! I'd love to see a runway model beat that! Well, this book was written to help you prepare your "infit" and get the best out of yourself everyday.

When we talk about what makes up your "infit", the amount of "infit's" you have on can be massive at times depending on how you feel and the circumstances surrounding you. Here is another example; you can wake up happy and ready to take over the world and then you put on something that makes you think of an unpleasant past experience and then you start to doubt your ability to take over the world! Or ladies you can put on an outfit that makes you feel as beautiful as Miss America, and once you look in the mirror you start to pay attention to a few minor flaws (according to what you view as flaws) and then you start to feel that you are more like Miss Ugly then Miss America! This is an example of how your "infit" can affect how you feel. Simple negative thoughts or ideas can cause a "wardrobe malfunction" quickly to your "infit".

One more example; have you ever met someone that was beautiful on the outside? I mean from head to toe. But they had an ugly disposition or were rude and unhappy? That was because their "infit" was not matching their "outfit". You see a lot of this in the entertainment industry! Beautiful models or actors just destroying their bodies with drugs and reckless behavior because their inside "infit" is in terrible shape.

I wrote this book to help people realize that you have to spend the same amount of time or more on your "infit" as you do on your "outfit". Value your inner wardrobe as much as you do your outer. When you look at the retail industry, people are spending top dollar for clothing. I know this for a fact because I just purchased a pair of jeans for the price of $$, well let me just say that it could have been a car payment for somebody! When did jeans become so expensive! Not to mention stores can not keep this certain brand of jeans in stock! That means they are flying off the shelves with a reckless abandonment. (Sorry I digress, just got a little excited). We can see by facts and figures that we spend a lot of money on looking good on the outside. But where are the numbers when it comes to your "infit." Here is how I measure the spending we do on our "infit." #1 Plastic surgery is at an all time high with over 8 billion dollars spent last year on cosmetic surgery. #2 Suicides are at a steady increase. #3 Self-help/self-esteem books are in high demand, and #4 Depression is becoming a normal way of living. If you go check these numbers out you would see that people are not really spending time on their "infit".

All of the things I just listed are triggered by a thought or feeling that originates on the inside. "I don't feel good about my nose so I am going to go get a new one!" "I hate my life so I want to leave this earth." "I feel I am not living at my full potential so I need to buy a book!" "I can not get over what happen to me last year so I think I am suffering from depression because of it!" Notice any reoccurring behavior in the four different statements? All of those statements started with a negative thought that could lead to a negative reaction. With a slight adjustment to your "infit" you could change every last one of those statements into a positive response which would lead to a positive reaction. That is what I hope to help you realize in this book. You can change the way you feel about yourself and your situation if you just get dressed from the inside!

Throughout this book you may see a few words or phrases you will not be familiar with. Have no fear in the back of the book you will find my own dictionary (Christopher's Dictionary)! Hey Webster has one why cant I!

I am not a preacher but I believe in God whole heartedly. Throughout this book I have a few spiritual moments where I drop Biblical references in. Don't be alarmed! Your belief system may be different than mine. And that is ok. Whether you believe in God or the Bible that is totally your call. I am not here to force feed you religion. But let me tell you something. When you look around and really check out what you see there can only be one Artist responsible. Guess who that is? God. That's right! Now it would not be right if I did not add my two cents. Hey that's what I am here for! I feel that if you climb aboard God's train you will be in for a ride full of love, prosperity, wealth, happiness, and good health! I don't know about you, but I got my ticket ASAP! I hope you will too. May this book bring you joy and happiness! I hope that if you can take anything away from my book it is that you are a beautiful work of art and God made no mistakes in making you, and you can do and be anything you want. All you have to do is believe in YOURSELF! May God bless you and your family always! Enjoy!

"God Is The Artist…. He Does Not Make Mistakes!"

WHEN I DECIDED to write this chapter I thought back to my most recent trip to a local art gallery. While I was checking the place out, I couldn't help but think that, some of the paintings were… how could I say… Ugly! Well, let me be polite and say that they were unpleasant to my eye. As I walked through the gallery "enjoying" the art, I'd occasionally find myself standing next to one particular lady who definitely saw something I could not see. I could tell by her responses, i.e *"Oh my God this is a Masterpiece and what a magnificent*

work of art!" I became even more freaked out when still another aficionado said; "I know exactly what the painter was trying to express at this point in the painting!" What was wrong with me that I could not see what they saw? Was I missing something? Were we even looking at the same piece of art? If you can't identify with what I am saying, put the book down right now! Whoa! Wait a minute, first read what I'd like you to do, then put the book down and follow the steps. If you've never been to an art gallery I invite you to do so right now. Go to your local gallery and drink it all in. Look at the art work and people around you. Watch how these people react to the paintings and or sculptures. Listen to their reactions. Pay special attention to reactions towards the pieces of art that you don't particularly like or that you think are down right ugly! See if others feel the same way. I guarantee somebody will see something beautiful or intriguing in a piece of art that looks like crap to you! Trust me they will. When you've had enough of this gallery experience come back, pick up my book and continue reading. That should prepare you for where I am about to go in this chapter! Go ahead I'll wait..................... (for those of you who have been to an art gallery and have an idea of what I am talking about take a bathroom break or go get a snack while we wait on them to come back). "Oh your back?" "How was it?" "Its not like they can really answer me!"

Let's continue. Now that we all are on the same page, take a moment to reflect on your art gallery experience. Some of us look at sculptures or works of art and the first thing we say is "hmmm." I say "hmmm" because I am trying to figure out what the *hockey puck* is going on in that piece of art. Most of us are trying to figure out what the artist was trying to accomplish. What messages are they trying to convey? Why did they put a red line in the middle of that blue painting? Or, why did they make one eye bigger then the other (shout out to Picasso)? We may not know who the painter is, but we do know that they must have been proud of their work. Proud enough to put it on display in a public setting.

In my quest to understand the mind of an artist when creating a masterpiece, I picked up a book by Robert Cumming through DK Publishing called *"Annotated Guides "Great Artist".* This book describes an artist more specifically a painter as; *"The type of personality that flourishes as a painter at any given time is the product of many different factors. There must be skill, determination, and inspiration, but these essential qualities are never enough in themselves. It is a simple truth that most artists reflect their own times but no more, whereas the outstanding artist has the ability to capture the imagination of future generations and say something of direct relevance to them. It is a rare occurrence and is possible only* **if the artist is working out of the deepest personal conviction with a wish to reveal something more than skill and with the intention to do more than impress or please an individual patron or a specific audience. The timelessness and universality of the work of a great artist exists because he or she has something exceptional to say, and because for such artist painting is not an end in itself but a means of trying to reach a fundamental truth.**" Think about that! If you need to put this book down and meditate on that for a minute or two go ahead and feel free. It's deep when you think of people like Picasso, Van Gogh, or Michelangelo who poured their hearts and souls into their work. Do we criticize them? Do we laugh at their final product? Maybe, I know I did. The answer should be no to both questions. Their art work reflects the greatness of the artist. What started as a blank canvas or lump of clay became a masterpiece in its own right. Are you still with me? I hope so.

Now who do you think is the artist of you? Not your parents because then you would have to ask who was the artist of them. To keep from doing all of that I have the answer! It's God! Yes, the big G.O.D. He is The Artist! Yeah I said it! For those of you who may believe God is a She we are not about to get into that debate. Let's just agree that to make man and woman, He has to have a little bit of both in Him! I want you too think about the excerpt from the book I just quoted to you (*the artist is working out of the deepest personal conviction with a wish to reveal something more than skill and with the intention to do more than impress or please an individual patron or a specific audience.*) I feel that explains our different shape's and colors. God was the first Artist! We are all different sizes and shapes. God was trying to do something different with each and every one of us!

I would like to try a little exercise. I want you to go to the nearest mirror. Before stepping in front of it, close your eyes and imagine the mirror is a blank canvas. Don't open your eyes until you have carefully positioned yourself in front of the mirror. When you open your eyes I want you to look at the work of art in front of you, as if you were in an art gallery. Check out the different features, colors, textures, shapes and hair. Take it all in! How do you feel? Are you happy? Sad? Disappointed? Ashamed? Do you cry? How have others responded to this piece of art before you? Do you say, "This is a *MASTERPIECE!*" Like the lady I described in the art gallery next to me. I would bet that most of you, reading this book, would not use the words *"MASTERPIECE"* to describe yourself. I am just now starting to understand that I am a *Masterpiece* and I am 29 years old!

Guess what? You are! You should yell at the top of your lungs, *"OH MY GOD, I AM A MASTERPIECE!"* Because you are! From the moment God created you, you were a Masterpiece! I imagine that when He was finished, He stepped back and said, *"Ah this is a MASTERPIECE!"* He made you to his exact specifications. No mistakes, no errors, no "I made a boo boo." He made a Masterpiece!

I feel that we sometimes don't appreciate who we really are when it comes to our outer appearance. In the Bible God said, *"Before I formed you in the*

womb I knew you (Jeremiah 1:5 NKJV). Formed...
There it is right there He just claimed that He is
The Artist. Every part of your body was designed
from the Man on High. When He formed you, I
feel He had the deepest personal conviction with
the wish to reveal something to someone! He says
"Be ye therefore perfect, even as your Father which
is in heaven is perfect (Matthew 5:48 NKJV).
Sorry, I had a moment! That leads me to believe
that we are perfect no matter what we look like.

Not everyone may agree with the perfection
of your *Masterpiece,* and it does not matter. They
are not God (The Artist).You are a *PERFECT*
work of art on display in HIS art gallery! Think
of the world as God's rotating art gallery. Now
think of all of the art He has on display. You are
in His collection. Take a look around and admire
some of His other art pieces. Do you remember
the example that I gave you earlier? How the
lady next to me found beauty in a piece of art I
thought was ugly. People see things differently all
the time. But no matter what others think when
they see God's Art... which is you. You have to
always see yourself as a *MASTERPIECE.* We
are all *MASTERPIECES* in God's eyes! He is
the Big Picasso. The Big Van Gogh in the sky!

Now go back to your mirror. You can even get naked this time if you want to. I don't suggest it but, hey whatever works for you (I am joking)! Follow the steps again. Look at every feature. Look at every line, shape, and color. Check out the textures and definitions of the artwork. Look at the Masterpiece in front of you. Scream out loud again (please try not to wake anybody up) "I am God's Masterpiece!" Say it over and over again, as many times as you need to until it starts to sink in. When you are done with that I want you to say, "God did not make a mistake on this work of art!" Say it! I want you to do one more thing before you walk away from your mirror. Say *"Thank You God!"* Go ahead I'll wait.......................

Did you do it? I hope you did! If you do this everyday in front of your mirror… (your picture frame), you will be able to appreciate what The Artist has done. You will be able to say job well done! Or as the lady in the art gallery said, *"Oh my God this is a MASTERPIECE!"* You could also say what I always say, "my compliments to The Artist!" I got that from listening to people at a fancy restaurant when they would say, "my compliments to the chef after eating a good meal!"

If you say any of the things that I have suggested to you, you will be improving your perception of the *Masterpiece* that God put you in charge of while you are here on this earth! Recognize that this is not Your body! Nope! You are merely the caretaker of God's art work. So you don't get to mess up the art! That's not why He gave it to you. He put you here to show off how great of an Artist He truly is! So what if someone doesn't appreciate the looks of your body! They are not the Artist. They just don't get what the artist was trying to say. They don't appreciate His style! So What! Somebody will. Just as the people in the art gallery saw the same picture and had different reactions, people will react differently to you.

When you put what you have viewed into prospective, you will begin to see how great God the Artist really is. You will understand that He does not make any mistakes. So today start looking at the *MASTERPIECE* in your mirror as God does! Pay attention to all of your details. See how you are divinely created. See where God put His touch of greatness. Say "I am a *MASTERPIECE*!" "I am God's work of art", and don't forget to finish with "Thank You, and Job well done, my compliments to the Artist!" Appreciate the art work God has created that is you. It's a lot better than the stuff down at your local art gallery with the six figure price tag! Trust me! There is no need to change the *MASTERPIECE* that is you. Love your art work as much as God does! Don't try to question the Artist about the artwork! Just admire it anyway!

Now I have to say this, your muscle and all of your physical attributes, or as I like to say, your ***"physical real estate"***, is just the frame around the art. If you are dieting or going to the gym, that's just like polishing the frame. You are also held accountable for damaging the frame by overeating, doing drugs or participating in any other risky behavior that may compromise the art work.

God may have intended for you to have a plump rump or He may have wanted you to be as soft as a teddy bear. He loves you as you are! Exactly the way He wanted you to be. Don't confuse going to the gym as messing with the artwork! Yes going to the gym may help mold the frame of the art work but remember being healthy requires a lot more than lifting weights. Make sure you are healthy on the inside as well. This is important. If you have a *brand new Mercedes body*, with a golf cart engine you will not benefit from the full experience of the *Mercedes*. You want to get the full benefit of your gift from God. Understand and love the *Masterpiece* He has given you. There is a reason He made you the way He did. You should not have any questions or concerns regarding your art work. Don't question it love it, the art work that is you! That is my new statement (*"Don't question it, Love it"*). Love every part of you! When you look at God's *Masterpiece*, remember just that! You are a *Masterpiece*! Once you appreciate the *Masterpiece* God has created for you, you will be able to start the process of getting dressed from the inside!

"Why Don't I Love Myself Consistently?"

I WILL START off with this question. Does the world we live in make you feel good about yourself? Wait, don't answer that just yet! Throughout this chapter I am going to touch on several reasons why we may not love ourselves consistently. We will look at how things beyond our control affect how we feel about ourselves. Put your seat belt on because it is about to get real in here.

I have been reading and reading research on our innate ability to love ourselves. I mean pouring over study after study, article after article, book after book; I think you get the point. I've been through new and old information, trying to figure out why love of self is not emphasized as much as it should be. I see that society emphasizes brotherly love and romantic love, but does very little in the self-love department. Here is my take on self–love. We don't love ourselves consistently because we know things about ourselves that others don't. Our inadequacies are the first things that come to mind. We can be fixated on the things we can't do, or the things we don't have to the point where we create a cycle of self-loathing. Once this cycle is created, it is not easy to destroy. I don't believe someone like, let's say, a doctor can help you love yourself. Not loving yourself is not like catching a cold or having a stomach virus. But we do have to fix this problem. We must find our own cure for this self-destructive behavior.

What is it that we all have in common? We all are in a state of constant learning and steady progress as human beings. Whether you're rich or poor we should be striving to become better at this thing called life. Sometime we can come up short when we try to branch out and try something new. And maybe we are not immediately good at our new endeavor.

Let me give you an example from my own life how I tried to become better at something. I am a pretty good cook (that's right I said it). Thanks to my mom! But I can not figure out microwave popcorn! Funny right? This is a very small problem right? You may even feel that although serious when it comes to movie night, my inability to cook microwave popcorn is not really a character flaw. I don't think I am judged for my inability to cook microwave popcorn. But this is an example of an area in my life where I come up short. We face things like this everyday of our lives, where we're dealing with some form of inadequacy. We all have things that we have trouble with, or have a hard time doing, and this may eat away at us. We can judge ourselves so harshly at times. No matter how small the task may be. I will admit, if I have a date or friends over to watch a movie, I will not be the first one to volunteer to show off my microwave popcorn cooking skills. And you know what? I am cool with that! Since I am ok with that, I can build a bridge and get over it. Because my "issue" is something as small as cooking popcorn, it seems that I should be able to get over this easily. Right? Well I did get over it eventually. The process I used to get over this was simple. I believe that if you try this process with your own problems you can get over them as well.

I have a few ideas on how to build a bridge to get over your problem. The most important thing to do is to release the idea that you lack something. Holding onto lack is never going to help you. You must embrace what you can do and what talents you do have. Enjoy and be grateful for your gifts. However, if it is truly your hearts desire to improve in an area that you lack in you must go for it no matter what the outcome may be! In the Bible it says "May He (God) grant you according to your hearts desire" (Psalm 20:4 NKJV). I will admit I did investigate the possibility of Emerald teaching a microwave popcorn cooking class! But to my disappointment he doesn't. It is not my heart's desire, so I can move on knowing I tried to better myself in the area I was lacking in. You get my point? If you really want to be good at something and it is your heart's desire, you have to try every avenue possible to increase your chances of success. If you are facing a challenge because you lack a particular skill then you have to try your hardest to enhance your ability to accomplish what you want to. Set your self up for success! Watch out here comes another spiritual moment;

In the Bible Jesus said "If thou canst believe, all things are possible to him that believeth" (Mark 9:23 NKJV). You must have the "desire" in your heart, and then you must "believe" you can do it, and then you must have "faith". Put it all together and go for it! Whether if you succeed or not you should not feel that you are inadequate in any way, as long as you put forth your best effort.

Now once you get over your inadequacies, you need to build yourself up on what you can do. This seems easy but most of us are taught to down play our strengths, accomplishments, successes and talents because we sound or can be considered conceited or narcissistic. Don't believe that, because it is a load of you know what! Do you celebrate your favorite actor or actress? Do you celebrate your favorite athlete? I know I do! No matter how small the accomplishment you cheer for them. Why not praise yourself for your accomplishments like you would for your favorite celebrity or athlete?

I live in Los Angeles, where I am fortunate enough to attend a few Laker basketball games a year. When Kobe Bryant (only the best player to ever play the game in my opinion) scores a basket, most of the people (including me) lose their minds! We scream at the top of our lungs as if he'd just found the cure for cancer. When he executes a reverse slam, you would think he'd just cured AIDS. I give you this example because I want you to seriously start to look at how you react to others that you may admire, or support, and cheer for them. Do you cheer like that for yourself? Do you have people cheering for you at work when you handle business? Do you get a standing ovation when you pass a class? Do you cheer like that when somebody shows an act of love by letting you over in traffic? I don't know of anybody that does, but these occurrences deserve as much applause and celebration as we give to our favorite celebrity or athlete. This type of practice will help you build yourself up. I am positive that the more you start to give yourself the support and admiration that you give to others it will benefit your "infit". You create a deficiency of love for yourself when you consistently down grade your accomplishments. I feel to Love yourself more you have to spend more time applauding the things you can do and less time on the things you can't do. When you are caught up in all the stuff you can't do you will overshadow the stuff you can do. Love yourself, embrace all that is you. Love your ability to care for others. Love your ability to make people smile. Love your ability to cook microwave popcorn! Giving yourself this type of affection will help you feel better about you and help you love who you really are.

Now let's take a deeper look at the word *Love*. Love is defined, by Merriam Webster's Collegiate Dictionary, as a strong affection for another, arising out of kinship or personal ties. The examples given are; maternal "love" for a child; "love" to play the violin; "love" for his schoolmates. Out of all the examples given for love and how to apply it, there are no references to love of one's self. There is more emphasis put on loving people and things outside of ourselves. I believe we should start a love festival within first. To truly love someone else you have to love yourself. Why wasn't that included in Webster's definition of love (check Christopher's Dictionary in the back of this book)? I do not have the answer and we can not blame Webster for that either! I decided to look at words that are commonly associated with the feelings for one's self. Narcissism; love of or sexual desire for one's own body. Then you have Conceit; excessive appreciation of one's own worth or virtue. These are words that not too many people want to be affiliated with when it comes to their identity. In this book I discuss the people on the wrong side of the spectrum of self-love. Those are the people that these definitions really apply to. I have to be bold here and say you are not wrong for loving yourself. In the Bible, God tells us to "love thy neighbor as thy self (Leviticus 19:18 NKJV)". Right there is the idea that we should love ourselves. You can tell who really belongs in the category of conceit and narcissism by the way they behave towards and react to others. They tend to keep all of that love to themselves. That is one side of the self-love spectrum. The other side is where you are trying to love yourself in order to love others. When you build yourself up and love yourself consistently, you will unleash a love inside of you that is transcendent to others. When you love yourself in this manner you are not in line with the dictionary's definition of self–love. When you have a balance you can love others as much as you love yourself. How do you attain this balance? You must cheer for yourself; love your abilities and talents! Once you do that then you can pass it on to others. When you can see the action of love for yourself, the attitude that comes with loving yourself in a positive light, you will begin to create a continuous stream of positive feelings and affirmations of yourself and your ability to love yourself and your ability to love others. This stream is essential in the journey of life and to loving yourself on a consistent basis.

How long have we camouflaged the fact that self-love is just as important as brotherly love or romantic love. I feel that if you love others and neglect yourself, you're not really helping yourself. This is also true if you love yourself and neglect others. You must think highly of yourself to give to the full extent of love. When you look at the dictionary it seems that loving yourself is such a negative thing. But loving yourself is the key to *getting dressed from the inside*. You have to love yourself. Once you love yourself, your inside "infit" will change and you will be able to share that love with others and not negate the love for yourself.

Remember from the first chapter, God created a MASTERPIECE in creating you. You are being selfish if you keep this love to yourself. But, when you are shining on the inside and you share that with others whether or not they give the same to you in return, you enhance your "infit". As you work to perfect your love for yourself, your love for others will grow as well. With the positive increase in both, you will experience enhanced love in your entire being.

When you strengthen your love of yourself from your inside "infit" the change will be evident, and it will be easier for you to decipher the appropriateness of what is considered normal in society and this world. You will be filled with love instead of being deprived of it. We try so hard to fit in, to love others, to please others, and to make others happy, that we hurt or neglect ourselves. If you would make the adjustment to love yourself first, you would see how little you are affected by your environment. Whatever is going on around you will not affect how you feel on inside. You are then in control of your inside "infit" and on your way to loving yourself in a consistent manner. If you allow your environment to dictate who you are then you are not in control of your "infit". We are individuals that posses many different talents and abilities. You are not defined by the initials on your purse or the letters on the sweater you wear or what car you drive. When you love yourself and get dressed from the inside with love and all of the other things you posses on the inside then your outside outfit will be nothing compared to how you look on the inside. This is not a hard thing to do. It is worth it, to become a better person inside and out! Here is something that I picked up while studying Nathaniel Braden, and his book "The Psychology of self-esteem." He says, (***"We are created to think, and we must do so in order to esteem ourselves highly. If we dim our awareness, or are passive or fearful, step by step we kill our greatest gift. The result is that we hate ourselves.) To love ourselves, we must cherish our ability to think."*** I have been trying to convey this message throughout this entire chapter. Mr. Braden refers to self-hate as a product of our own creation! If you don't love yourself consistently, it is due to you. You must love yourself, and continue to love yourself every chance you get. When you've finished this book and followed the examples I have given you, you will feel an inward shift. One that is an indication of your "infit" coming together. Then you will be able to see why you have not been loving yourself consistently and make the change necessary to do so!

"It's Time For A Change!"

ALFRED ADLER, A well known psychologist said something that was as true during his era (the early part of the 1900's), as it is today. He said, ***"The hardest thing for a human being to do, is to know themselves and to change themselves."*** I agree with him. Most of us know where we are challenged. And what we need to do to meet it head on, but we can't always, muster up the courage or energy to do it. Since Mr. Adler made this wise statement, we have put a man on the moon and created a car that can parallel park itself (shout out to Lexus). But we can't fix ourselves! I find that funny. We have to know ourselves to fix ourselves. We can get caught up in going along with the program and lose sight of who we are on the inside. Therefore when it is time to change something on the inside (do a rewiring as I call it) we don't know where to start or how to change. Although this is not that true for the outside. After checking the latest cosmetic surgery statistics, that show that there were over 13 million procedures done in 2006, netting the cosmetic surgery industry revenues estimated somewhere in the ball park of 8 billion dollars. This clearly shows how committed most of us are to changing our outward appearance. Are we as committed to changing ourselves from within? Thank God for putting a pad lock on the physical aspects of our bodies! Because if he didn't most of us would be ordering body parts like we were at an all you can eat buffet! "I'll take a new chin, longer legs, and a new nose to go please!" Funny, I know, but just meditate on this for a moment. You can only do so much to change your outward appearance, but you can change all kind of stuff on the inside! You can change your mind, your feelings, and your attitude! You can also make yourself forget negative memories. If you wanted to, you could make yourself think the color blue was really red! Ok, that's taking it kind of far, but you get my point. We can change how we think and feel about ourselves! It can be done. You can change! In the Bible, God says "Strip yourselves of your former nature… and be constantly renewed in the spirit of your mind [having a fresh mental and spiritual attitude] Ephesians 4:22, 23 (AMP).

Here is a key how to get started renewing your mind right away! You must change any negative feelings you have towards yourself as soon as possible. Especially if these negative feelings prevent you from loving yourself. I want you to see that in order for you to start loving yourself fully you have to examine any negative thoughts or ideas you may have about yourself that could prevent you from loving you. You could be your own worst enemy. If you are guilty of tearing yourself down for whatever reason, may it be in your "short coming's", or inadequacy as we discussed in the last chapter how this negative behavior can lead to your unhappiness, you have to stop the cycle. That, I am sorry to say, is very self-destructive behavior.

It is time to change! Create your own restoration team instead of your current demolition team! Restore what has been lost in the tearing down process you have been use to! Everybody can change!!!

"Parents Pick Our Inside Wardrobes Early In Our Lives."

FROM THE TIME we are born our brain is soaking up everything around us. Everything that we are soaking up will determine how we will proceed through life. Our parents have a very strong influence during this process. It is obvious that our parents are our initial link to the world, the society we live in, and our heritage during our dependent years (from birth until we are 18). Everything that they expose us to whether good or bad will make up the majority of our inside wardrobe we will use in our adulthood. When I say wardrobe in keeping with the theme of this book it means your emotions, beliefs, morals, and pretty much the blue print for how you will be in life. The wardrobe our parents give us is not always bad. But there are times where we are affected negatively by our parents "infit". In this chapter, I am going to discuss a couple of ways that parents may have affected you're inside wardrobe.

One way our parents influence our internal selves is by passing on their insecurities and short comings (as if they were a great inheritance). The second way parents may affect us in a negative way is they indelibly influence our career paths. We all are asked "what do we want to be when we grow up?" How many parents actually assist their children in pursing the career they want? The last area I want to discuss is a very sticky area. I know many parents that aren't concerned with what their child(ren) may want in a mate. They are only concerned in the mates they want for their child(ren)!

Let's tackle the transfer of insecurities and short comings that can happen between parent and child. When parents project their own insecurities and short comings onto their children, it can create a child who is fearful and filled with insecurities that they did not ask for. Here is a side note; "as much as you may love your parents you are not them". Just because you come from them does not mean that you are automatically limited to what they were or are limited to. Think about it for a second. Also think about things that you have heard them say they can't do, or wish they could do, don't have etc. Somehow without you even trying, you already feel you have the same issues, or the odds are stacked up against you.

Here is an example where I was affected in my life by that very situation. My mother always reminded me that she was not athletic. She figured that since she was a great singer, I would also be better at singing than at sports. Let me be the first to tell you, if you don't already know, we don't always inherit our parent's talents and abilities. This can be a difficult thing for some parents to deal with. You know the old saying "chip off the ol' block." Parents may feel that because they excel at something their child should also (placing their expectations on the child). Or, if the parent feels they are deficient in an area, they may automatically believe that their child is also.

In my case, I can't sing my way out of a paper bag, but I was an All-State athlete and I made it to the State Championship in Track & Field every year in high school. I played high school varsity in every sport except soccer. See how that could have been disastrous for me? If I would have accepted my mom's abilities and shortcomings as my own, I would have missed out on one of my true passions, athletics. Please do not judge your parents by their shortcomings and insecurities. You should use them as a way to save yourself some grief about your own perceived strengths and weaknesses. What maybe a challenge for your parent's maybe an area of strength for you and vice versa. Even though my mom's shortcomings were in my sub-conscious, I did not claim them as my own, I used them as inspiration. By not claiming her fears about her inability to be athletic, I was able to play the sports that I enjoyed and loved, and excelled in. If I had allowed her fears to consume me they could have squashed my desire to play sports.

Here is one more example. This time I will use something my father had trouble with that I did not. My father passed away before I was born. I was always told that my father had an undeniable unhappy disposition. He always seemed to be upset and mad at the world. But that was not my case; I may have gotten his nose and ears but not his mentality. I was always a happy child. It is clear to me that I did not inherit this from my father. I wanted to share this with you because I hear people say that they are just like their parents when it applies to certain negative behavior. I am here to say that you do not have to be like them.

Facing your parent's challenges on a daily basis could easily effect one's way of thinking and seep into their natural potential to be great. I was able to succeed in areas where my parents did not.

How have your parents dealt with their inner challenges. Do they love themselves fully? Do they know how? Think about it. In the past there were not as many books or therapeutic ways to help a person work on or change their self-image. It may be possible that our parents may not have been open to, or had the ability to deal with their inner issues.

If this is your case in order to start healing you will need to disassociate yourself from any negative tendency your parents may have passed on to you. If you don't, you will be keeping yourself from achieving your goals and dreams. And at the same time holding yourself back from doing something that you are more than capable of doing.

Age is not a factor. If there are any dreams or aspirations that you have let go, or did not pursue because of your parents. It is time to change that (if you need help changing re-read chapter 3 again). Reprogram yourself then go after them! Try something different, something you may not have thought you could do before, because your parents could not do it. You can even try an old thing that you have been doing, but in a different way! I must reiterate this is not a dig on parents at all. This is a way for you to be accountable for yourself now. You are not your parents. You may have come from them but you are not them. We must respect and love our parents for bringing us into this world. But we have to be accountable for what happens once we become adults. We are in control of our "infit" now!

It is important that you realize what you want for yourself, and what your parents want for you. These are two very different things at times. I am not saying that parents are right or wrong for wanting what they want for you, but the ultimate decision, of what can happen for you, is yours.

This same approach should play clear for your career path as well. But most often times that is not the case. In my opinion the Cosby Show (from the 80's) was a perfect example of how a successful parent/child relationships should work, when it comes to the career choice you will make. There was a father (who was a doctor), and a mother (who was a lawyer). None of their kids followed in their professional foot steps (even though we don't know how Rudy ended up). I think that Sondra their oldest daughter did go to medical school (but I think she ended up opening a wilderness store with her husband, I am not sure I had a very early bedtime). These parents showed that even though they wanted their children to follow in their footsteps, by following some family traditions (i.e. attending their alma mater or major in the same field), they still encouraged their children to choose their own paths and walk them. Some parents are not like this. Some want to control every aspect of their child(ren)'s life. They thrive on living vicariously through their children. This type of relationship does have its benefit. If a child decides he or she wants to pursue a career that their parent has excelled in, and or has experience in, their parent can be very instrumental in creating a positive outcome. I believe we all need and can benefit from guidance and mentoring, but only if it can assist us in the direction we want to go. Trust me, I am happy I decided to take the path I chose, and I have a mother that supported my choices (most of the time, ha). I am joking about most of the time. Even if she did not agree with a certain decision of mine she did not judge me. She allowed me to make my own decision; she just would kindly remind me that I would have to deal with the consequences either way! If I hadn't, I may have ended up a singer and baker (my mom can throw down in the kitchen as well), in Kansas City!

When you become an adult, parents have to give you room to grow. This is the space we need to show what we've learned. Also to show how much we love ourselves and appreciate what they have done for us. This is a very important part of parenting. We need to look at the picture our parents painted for us and see where our goals and dreams may differ from theirs. Once that has been done, we need to see if any adjustments need to be made. If we are not on the path we want to be on, we can change it up, and still live a positive and productive life regardless of whatever prior limitations you think you may have.

Here we are at the dating portion of this chapter. I have a lot of experience in this area and many examples to share, because, I am a momma's boy, and my mother's opinion of my significant other matters to me. There was a time when my mom's idea about who I dated wasn't important. And I have dated a few young ladies that their parents were not to fond of the fact I was dating their daughter. So I have been on both sides of the coin.

Here is one example of how a parent may influence their child's dating preference because of the parent's insecurities, hidden agendas, or past experiences. This example is from one of my past relationships. My ex-girlfriend's dad wanted her to marry a wealthy star athlete. He was very adamant about this subject. So much so that he forced his daughter into situations she did not necessarily want to be in but did it because of his approval. I asked myself why he was this way. Her father didn't have any of those qualities he wanted her to look for in a potential mate. He was a 5'5", assembly line blue collar worker, who beat his wife and was generally miserable. How was he qualified to make this very important decision regarding her happiness? Why not let her make her own decision? Why give her a narrow minded view of the opposite sex as it relates to the ideal man for her? I guess he didn't want her to suffer like her mother had with him. Whatever his reason, he had programmed her to look for a rich athlete (football star) no matter how he treated her. He was setting her up for failure when he could have been teaching her to succeed in an area he had no success in. He could have told her to look for more lasting and intrinsic values than money or status. This is how a parent can drop the ball when it comes to preparing their child for the future when it comes to dating. Now, my mom is the exact opposite. My mom taught me that as long as you find someone that has your back and your best interest at heart you should pursue them. Oh, I left out, and they must love God! See how my mother instilled in me something that I can use on a broad perspective. She did not give me tunnel vision, like my ex girlfriend's father gave her! Regardless of how your parents feel about who you date, if you find someone who lines up with your dreams for your life, and at the same time maintains their own dreams goals and aspirations, then you have found the one for you!

That's why you have to release the wardrobe your parents selected for you if it is not helping you achieve your dreams and goals. Your "infit" and your wardrobe for it can be reprogrammed when it comes to your career, goals, dreams, what you believe and your dating preference. It has to be if it is hindering you. If you find that you have been limited by your parents, you must shed that influence, and find the best way to uncover, and discover your dreams, desires, hidden talents or abilities. Do what you can to discover you, to know you, and love you. Parents should allow their children to discover what makes them happy! Do whatever it takes to make sure you are in control of your "infit" and your views of who you really are. It's your responsibility! This only applies to those of you who feel that your parents have had a negative affect on you and your "infit". Most parents don't mean any harm, but sometimes they can't see where their behavior has been harmful to your mental and emotional growth. If this is your situation, you have to take the reins of your life. And remember, only one person is in control of your inside "infit", and that is you.

"I Am The Most Beautiful Woman In The World Inside And Out!"

WHEN I FIRST thought of this chapter, I was coming from a place of anger towards women. I had just got out of a relationship where I thought I was with the woman of my dreams.

From the first time we met I felt she was the one for me, because on the outside she was everything I wanted and more! She appeared to be just as beautiful on the inside. She was into God. She knew just what to say and just when to say it. She liked sports, and she was athletic. She spoke about marriage and having my child, and she even purchased me a wedding ring. I was so in love it was coming out my ears (yes I have big ears, so what, ha)! But little did I know that deep down inside of this seemingly flawless woman I would find a broken, abused, low self-esteem, pessimistic person.

She was one of the most incredible people on the outside, everybody loved her. I could not see that she was just putting on a show to hide her true self. In the middle of planning for a wedding and the birth of my daughter, I started to see signs of her battered "infit". Her "infit" could not be disguised anymore. I could not believe that I would discover that this beautiful woman that could have any man in the world was truly suffering from a past of domestic violence, child abuse, self-hate, low self-esteem and she had no value of her true self.

As time went on and more and more of her true self started to emerge, I stood strong and was not going to let go. I felt that she could get over her past if she had someone to really love her. I knew the only way I could help her, was to love her with all my heart. But I was so wrong. She was so wounded by her parents and past broken relationships that she did not know how to love herself. The more I tried to love her and show her she was worth more than gold to me, the more she continued to self–destruct. The more she would self–destruct on the inside, the more she would pull on her outer appearance to compensate for the lack of inner love she so desperately needed to create. I finally got the picture that no matter what I could or would do, I could never repair her torn heart and bandage up her inner scars. I tried so hard to get her to look at herself the way that I did. I saw her through the eyes of God! I saw her potential to be a loving person. I wanted her to know how beautiful she was despite her tragic and tormented past. No matter how I tried to show her this, she would just turn away and ignore me. I could see she was going to continue on this downward spiral into a pit of self-hate. Here is a side note; I have to add that women love compliments, but in order to receive the compliment you have to realize you have something to compliment. I saw her true potential and that she could be and do anything she put her heart and mind too. I did not realize until we had broken up, not only was I sad that I could not help her, but I also found out that my mission to save her was useless, because she did not know how to change her "infit". Throughout all of this I found out that her story of the miscarriage of my daughter was a lie, and she actually had an abortion. I could not believe that she deceived me and kept that locked up inside of her for so long. That had to be eating her up on the inside as well. I could only attribute that behavior to a person who suffered from a torn and battered inside. So, I made a vow to myself and God. I would first forgive her in my heart and in my mind. Second of all, I would ask God for forgiveness for anything that I did wrong. And finally, I would spend the rest of my life making sure any woman I came into contact with knew how important she was and how beautiful she was inside and out regardless of her past or insecurities! That is why this chapter is so important to me. I wanted to give you an example of my first hand experience with someone who had no idea of her true self-worth.

In this chapter, I am going to list everything possible to show women that they have so much more to them than just their bodies (or *physical real estate*). Body parts will eventually sag and wrinkle but your "infit" will always be beautiful if you choose to have it that way.

Ladies I need you to know that you are unique! Regardless of what Hollywood tries to make you think about your outer appearance. I have to state this fact again, last year there was over 8 billion dollars made in the cosmetic surgery industry (statistics from The World Almanac 2007). I believe we are having surgery on the wrong thing! We should be *"implanting"* love, knowledge and appreciation to our "infit". I feel we should be *"reducing"* harmful memories that affect our attitude towards ourselves. I feel we should be *"botoxing"* our hopes and dreams to enhance them! We should be *"uplifting"* each other! I cannot stress this enough, there is only one you! There is no one else on this planet like you! That is a fact! There may be a person who you have similarities with but nonetheless you are not the same. Let me ask you a question, can you name five things about your "infit" that no one else has? I bet you can name five things about your physical real estate that someone else has. I feel that some ladies (and this is just my opinion) spend so much time trying to fit in and be what society considers normal that they lose their true identity.

What are you doing to make sure you are unique and reaching your full potential? What are you doing to make sure everyone you come in contact with realizes your unique self? What are you doing to make sure you are not penalizing yourself for any reason? Do you think you are pretty? Are you happy with yourself?

I can talk about this all day. I know way too many women that are not getting the most out of their lives, because their "infit" does not match up with their outfit.

You should not be trying to compete with other women. I feel that everyday women are bombarded with reminders of what they don't look like or what they should look like. I want to let you know that the only competition you should be in is making this world a better place through an act of love and kindness! Not your outfit! If you expose your "infit" at its best then there is no competition at all! Since you are unique and we all are different, then there is no way some one can be better than you at being you! Get it? The only way that can happen is if you put yourself into a category that can be judged. If you try to compete with your physical real estate, you will be judged. Even though you are a *MASTERPIECE*! I end this chapter by giving you some free clothing (everybody loves free clothes)! Not for your "outfit" but for your "infit"! You are; nurturing, lovely, beautiful, smart, a sweet smelling rose, stunning, ecstasy, gorgeous, alluring, attractive, pretty, delightful, glamorous, graceful, elegant, and exquisite! For you to think anything less would be a terrible misfortune! I love you even though I do not know you!

"I am THE CHAMP!"

WHEN I WAS writing this book, I thought this would be the easiest chapter to write, because I am a man! Boy was I wrong! Our "infit" is just as complex as a woman's. We are taught that guys are simple; TV, sports, money and a women is pretty much how we tick! I can only speak from what I was taught and the images I see on TV. If this does not apply to you, I understand. I could not really believe that was it! I got out the dictionary and started to search for what a man was defined as. In Webster's Dictionary and Thesaurus here are the words I found that would be a part of how we were described on the inside; brave, courageous, fearless, firm, heroic, lion hearted, audacious, tenacious, indomitable, noble, valiant, bold, confident, self-reliant, independent, stand alone, and protective. That is not that simple is it? After reading all that, I tried to come up with one phrase that we can say to ourselves that will start our process of getting dressed from the inside that can encompass all of those words! That phrase is... "I AM THE CHAMP!" When I wake up in the morning I say this to myself. I feel that I am the champ of my emotions, my mental status, my confidence, my love, and my life! I can conqueror anything. I will not let anyone take that from me. MANLY HUH! As men we have to get up for the day in a way that we are in total confidence of our situation no matter what may be going on around us. As I tried to figure out the best way to share this to my champions reading this book, I thought I should first explain what a champ really is.

Webster's Dictionary defines Champ as; champion. Champion is defined in the same dictionary as; (1) Warrior, Fighter. (2) Defender. (3) One who does battle for another's rights or honor. (4) a winner of first place in competition; also one who shows marked superiority. Now most people think of a champ as a sports figure. I would admit that I did too also before I took a look at the definition. Don't get me wrong a champion of the sports world is definitely something to admire.

I have a few friends who have won a championship in some sport. My friend Chris "Peto" Hayes won a super bowl with the Green Bay Packers. I admired him for his accomplishment, but I wondered what made him different than me? For starters, that huge super bowl ring on his finger. Secondly, the experience he had received from playing in the NFL. But that was it. When I saw how well he treated his family and how he handled his business that is where I saw the true champion in him. And then I thought, "Wow we are all champions." Everyday we live and try to provide, support and help others.

Be a champ at work, be a champ in traffic (by letting somebody over or not getting angry if you get cut off). Be a champ by loving and helping out the less fortunate. "Peto" won his championship on a football field in front of a large audience. Well my new champions your stage and field is everyday life once you put your feet on the floor when you get out of bed! As Chris Hayes says in his book,

"Suits On, Game ON"! You are a champion! You have to think that way, in order to get the most out of your "infit". Think of your "infit" as a uniform, before you get in the game your uniform must be on!

I am going to leave you with this my new champions. I will use football as an example but all other sports have equipment as well. Your typical football uniform has; shoulder pads, helmet, mouth piece, thigh pads, shoes, socks, cup, tailbone pad, gloves, jersey and pants. Well my newly crowned champions here is your "infit" uniform; Confidence (I can do all things through Christ who strengthens me, Philippians 4:13 NKJV), Self-esteem (I am a great, strong, and wise man. I am high in my own self-esteem so I may be able to look out for others), Goals (I will not take a detour, I will go straight ahead at my goals, I will complete them and see them through the end no matter what the outcome may be), Dreams (I will look forward to the future and plan to be better then I am now), Strength (I am strong in spirit and mind regardless of my physique or my outer appearance. I will stand strong on my word and have strength to finish anything I start. In the Bible God says "Let the weak say, "I am strong" [A warrior] (Joel 3:10 (AMP) I AM STRONG, I AM A WARRIOR), Attractive (I am attractive to my future and my goals. They think I am beautiful! I will do my best to make sure they both look good at all times). Remember the Bible tells us that "for as he thinks in his heart, so is he" Proverbs 23:7 (NKJV). So when you say "I AM THE CHAMP" think and feel that you are in your heart and your "infit" will reflect it!

"You Are Too Cute To Act So Ugly!"

❦

I USED TO laugh when my grandmother, Essie Lee Johnson aka "Nanny", would say "You are too cute to act so ugly". She would say this whenever I would cry or pout about something I could not do or get. You know, when kids throw tantrums in the cereal aisle at the grocery store, because they want frosted flakes instead of corn flakes? That is when they are acting ugly. This applies to adults as well. You could be looking marvelous on the outside, but if your inside feelings don't match up with your outside appearance, then there is bound to be some type of disconnect. You must understand that thoughts determine your actions, your attitudes, and your self-image. If you think negative in anyway about your "infit", that thought will affect your emotions, your attitudes and eventually your actions. You don't want to give the wrong impression, right?

When I think of what kind of example I can come up with to help you see my point visually, I think of a cute panda bear. They're so adorable; I just want to hug them. They are not growling or lashing out. They are just sitting there minding their own business. They seem so serene, but as soon as you get close they try to eat you alive. No dig on the pandas but that is just the truth. People can be the same way. They may look approachable, sweet as pie, and then you get too close, or speak to them, and they bite your head off. That is because some where inside of them a negative thought has turned into negative actions. Don't be that way. Allow your outer appearance to reflect your inner self.

If you are constantly bombarded by negative critical thoughts that may influence the way you think about yourself you must change those thoughts. The Bible says, be "transformed by the

renewing of your mind" Romans 12:2 (NKJV).
You have to make sure you're "infit" is always a
reflection of positive, fruitful thoughts. That way
you will not have to hear someone yell out, "You
Are Too Cute Too Act So Ugly!"

"Don't Let The Package Fool You! It Could Be An Empty Box!"

I HAVE LIVED in several beautiful cities including Miami and Los Angeles. I have had the good fortune of being around some of the most beautiful people in the world. I have worked in the entertainment industry, specifically Radio and Television for 13 years, so I have come in contact with beautiful actresses, models, performers, and entertainers. I wanted to know what their appeal was. I am not just talking about their outer beauty. I wanted to know, what about these people would make woman, and men alike do anything to be in their presence. I could never figure it out. I would speak to them and hold a conversation, and they seemed like regular people. I paid extra close attention to the women, of course. They were beautiful on the outside. I mean, all the right curves, all the right physical real estate. Face, Back Sides, Breast, Legs, Eyes, Hair! They had very good physical real estate! And oozing sexuality! Just SEXY! I figured that it must be their outer appearance that draws people to them. In other words their packaging!

But what was disturbing was that 90% of those women that I came in contact with, including my ex fiancé, were hiding inner demons, even the likes of which Satan would be hesitant to fight! The packaging fooled me! It was an empty box, better yet imagine the most hideous monster you can think of... Let me help you out! Picture the Predator mixed with Grace Jones, (not the Grace Jones character in Boomerang because she was Hot in that movie, but her early movies) and Medusa. Put that all together. Got it? Can you see it? Good. Now that is how the 90% looked on the inside to me. I mean some of the most eye catching women I have met in the world appeared like that gruesome character on the inside. You may ask me, "How can you tell Christopher?" "Did you have special glasses on or are you superman with x-ray vision?" No. But I could tell by the way they treated themselves. By how they acted when the cameras were not around, and by how they allowed others to treat them.

I wondered what would make something so beautiful (on the outside of course) be so ugly on the inside? I found myself asking this question almost daily when I was with my ex during our relationship. I have come up with a few reasons why they may be this way.

They may have gone through things that nobody should have to endure such as; physical, verbal, sexual, or emotional abuse. Or they could have been ugly as a child or obese, and were bullied or picked on and still carry that shameful memory as baggage.

There could be a number of reasons why they acted the way they did. But-none-the-less it was totally the opposite of their outer appearance. If you are a victim of any of the things that I have listed you may be hiding inner demons as well that need to be released.

If so there are many ways to address any of these issues. A counselor may need to be consulted, or check out this suggestion from yours truly. FORGET ABOUT IT! That's right let it go! Build a bridge and get over it. Let it go how you were, or what you saw, or how you were treated in your past. Let it go! Pray to God to forgive those who have wronged you! Then ask God to ease the pain that those memories may cause in you. And then ask God for a spirit of forgiveness to fall upon you!

I can hear some of you now! "It is not as easy as you make it sound Christopher!" YES IT IS!!! Now I am a person that looks to help as many people as possible in their time of need but I can't help everyone. I suggest if you are a person that has trouble with letting go, you should seek help like I said early. Get into a support group of some kind, a church preferably. Seek people that have been through what you have been through. Most people think they are weak if they seek help. Some don't want to talk to strangers about their personal business, or they are just down right embarrassed to speak about certain things in their past. Sometimes it's through a doctors words or encouragement that you may see the light or the solution to help you move forward. It helps to talk out loud about something you have been fighting on the inside by yourself. Get it out! You will feel better. A great friend of mine is a well known psychologist in California. Dr. Perri Johnson is not only a great Psychologist but he is one of my spiritual advisors. He has told me about several studies that show that patients, who forgave their attackers or offenders, healed better mentally and physically than those who did not forgive. That is scientific research people! You have to forgive who ever may have hurt you in your past, in order to have a better chance at getting over any pain they may have caused that still affects you. It will not hurt to try! In the Bible, God tells "Repay no one evil for evil" (Romans 12:17 NKJV). If you have been a victim of someone's evil ways whether on purpose or not, you not only need to let what they did to you go, but you also have to forgive them as well. You don't even have to forgive them face to face. Forgive them in your heart and watch how letting go becomes a little easier. You could even write them a letter and tell them how you feel! You don't even have to send it to them. Whatever it takes to help you get over the negative issue, which is affecting you.

Back to the ladies! All of these women I mentioned could stop traffic. I should know (my ex fiancé did it a couple of times). But, no matter what they received because of their outer appearance, may it be a compliment or Gucci, or someone saying "you are wearing the heck out of that dress," they did not benefit on the inside. They still were the same damaged, misguided, wounded soul on the inside.

I can tell you that when you feel good on the inside it will be reflected on the outside. If you can coordinate your "infit" with your outfit you will be on your way to making sure your packaging is not covering an empty box or an ugly gift. You have to find the balance that can bring you the happiness necessary to affect your "infit".

"The Bottled Water Theory."

༄

I CAME UP with a theory while studying the psychology of the human being. What drives us? What makes us tick? I found out some very interesting things. The overall consensus was; human contact, affection negative and positive. Put that all together and you have human interaction is pretty much what I got from every great psychologist that I studied. We have some type of human interaction everyday. This interaction may it be positive or negative can affect your "infit." Think about it for a second...

Look at all human interaction you are in everyday. The compliments you receive, positive comments you may receive, the accolades you may receive, social acceptance and then look at the negative comments you may receive, the judgmental comments, the rude comments, as *Water* you receive from the individuals you come in contact with. A few examples are; "you are beautiful", "you are smart", "you did a great job", "you are great", "you are the best". Think of all the human interaction that you receive through out your day as "Water" or the exchange of "Water".

Before you leave your house each day you have the chance to fill up with your own water.

Imagine that when you walk out the door each day that everywhere you go throughout your day, there are people trying to give you a taste of their water, no matter if the "Water" is positive (good water) or negative (tainted water) . I don't know if you've experienced a marathon, but if you have watched a marathon, there are points in the race where people line up holding cups of water out for the runners. The runners grab one or two cups to quench their thirst, or cool their bodies down. All of those people on the side lines with cups of water are there to make sure the runners are hydrated and the race flows. Follow me? Now picture yourself with the same setup as you go into the world on your daily journey. When you go to work, the grocery store, school or church, pretty much everywhere you go, imagine people standing there holding bottles of water for you. Since we all need water, we take a drink of their water (which is listening to what they have to say). Well we have to because we need to remain hydrated (hydrated means the need for human interaction) throughout the day and they need to offer in order to keep the flow going in your daily race. Get my drift? Man this is good stuff. Thank You God! Well if you don't fill up on water before you leave home or bring your own water bottle you will find yourself controlled by other people's water. Or in layman's term, what other people think about you. This is where your "infit" could change for the worst. If you fill yourself up with negativity, bias opinions and just other people's own self destructive ideas of them that they project on you, you start to get confused. This should never happen. Why? Because you are in control of how you feel about yourself. Take a drink of your own water when someone tries to give you negative tainted water.

You have your water bottle with you right? When some one says "you suck!" Spit out that **Water** (mentally, do not actually spit on them, play nice) and drink your own **Water** by saying "No I don't, I am a great individual!" It is true we do need human interaction but we should and can receive this without sacrificing our inside "infit". If you feel good on the inside you will look good on the outside no matter what anybody has to say. They will not affect you because you are drinking your own water. Get it? You fill yourself up on your own happiness, and your own acceptance. You will find no matter what somebody says about you, you are already full of your own water. You know you look good. You know you're a good person. You know you are a hard worker. Regardless of what they may think.

At the end of the day you are full of your own untainted water. Once you utilize this theory you can see where you can survive off of your own water and get rid of any negative tainted water you receive. There are people all over this world waiting to say something negative or to harm someone with their words. Those people don't love themselves. That is the only reason they do what they do. You have to fill up with your own good water! Then when you are the person giving out water (because you will) you will be able to give out the good water that you have in yourself and that way you will not be one of those people giving out tainted water!

"Ladies and Gentlemen You Too Can Be Like The Sun and The Moon?"

THIS IS A crazy title for a chapter. But, as I was writing this book, I was sitting outside by the pool just enjoying the sun. Then this thought popped into my head. The sun and the moon have the same routine everyday. They both make their way across the sky everyday in the same pattern! Even though they do the same thing everyday, some days are brighter or hotter than others, and sometimes the moon is full and sometimes it's not. If you go into space (please don't try to) the moon and the sun are round and the same all the time. They are the same shape (circle) all the time and travel the same path. Rise in the East set in the West.

Let's look at what do we do on a consistent basis in our life.

Most of us wake up in the morning and hit the alarm clock. Well some of us do. We go to the bathroom, brush our teeth use the bathroom, and take a shower (some of us do ha, ha). We eat breakfast and then we start our day. Some of us drive to work or school, the same way, using the same streets or highways everyday. Even though this is a routine we are still not like the sun and moon in our actions. Weekends we may not follow the same order, and on holidays we may have a change in our routine. Now let's look at night time. Some of us brush our teeth, get in our pajamas, say our prayers (everyone should be doing that), and we hit the sack. That is still not consistent like the moon (sometimes you sleep and sometimes you don't). Ok so we all see that even the most redundant habits we have almost everyday we still don't do them consistently like the sun and moon.

Here is something you can start today that will be similar to the routine that the sun and the moon have. If you add this slight adjustment into your daily schedule, and do it consistently like the sun and the moon do, you will be on your way to keeping a highly maintain "infit". You can do this and you should do this everyday no matter how you're feeling. No matter how your schedule is adjusted.

Here is what I would like you to do. When you wake up in the morning, and at night before you go to bed, I want you to look in the mirror, (it does not matter if it is the one in the kitchen, the bathroom, or your bedroom). On your mirror you should put a list of things you love about your "infit". Make a list from the tools I have given you in this book. Now be as original as possible. Try to make your list as detailed as possible to who you really are. Make sure you use the examples I have given you . This should not be hard because God has given you a lot in your Masterpiece to love! When you look at your mirror I want you to say these things out loud. So you can hear the words come out of your mouth. Believe them and mean them. In the Bible, God says that "Death and life are in the power of the tongue" Proverbs 18:21

(AMP). What you say can control the direction of your life!

Here are a few examples of how your list could look; I am loved, I am smart, I am beautiful, I am setting my mind in the right direction, Goodness and Mercy are following me all day long! I have the favor of God with everyone I come in contact with. As you can see the majority of things listed are mental nuggets that can build up your "infit". I also suggest putting pictures up on the mirror that remind you of happy times in your life. I am a strong believer in many forms of positive reinforcements. Pictures that are nostalgic and bring back happy memories set off an explosion of energy that is positive and can have an instant affect on how you feel about yourself at that particular time. I don't care what you put up on the mirror as long as it is positive and can help you get to a place mentally where you will be open enough to where you can start the process of "Getting Dressed From The Inside!"

Make time for this ritual everyday! I want you to really believe the words that are coming out of your mouth. When your "infit" is together then your "outfit" will reflect that!

I can not stress this enough! This is a very important part of the process to insure you are "Getting Dressed From The Inside!"

The sun and the moon are your friendly reminders that your ritual should be initiated. When you wake up the sun is there, think about it, take a glance at it (don't stare right at it, duh) and do your ritual. Before you go to sleep look outside, the moon will be your reminder to do your ritual again.

Now you have a constant reminder to do your ritual. Even if it's cloudy where you are on a particular day, you still know the moon and sun are hard at work doing their routine, so you should be right with them during your routine!

This process of filling yourself up with love of your character, happiness about who you are, and joy about what you can do, and gratitude for what you have done, will start to connect with the inner you and start to control how you look to yourself on the inside! Trust me, I do this process everyday and I am 29 years old and I find out more about me to love everyday. I find a new way to appreciate my ears or my lips, and my personality. When you fill yourself up with positive things like this every night and day, you will have no choice but to change you're inside "infit".

From that moment on, you will have a constant reminder of how much of a wonderful "infit" you have on! You can now be at your full potential and get out there and make a difference in the world!

I wanted you to know that I love you as my brother and sister in Christ! Thank you for allowing me to speak to you for a while. I hope you succeed in everything you do from this point on in your life. There can only be one you on this earth! Try everyday to make sure you are the best you can be. May God Bless You & Your Family ALWAYS!

Scripture References

Scripture Reference;
Leviticus 19:18 New King James Version
 Psalm 20:4 New King James Version
Proverbs 18:21 AMP
Proverbs 23:7 NKJV
Jeremiah 1:5 New King James Version
Joel 3:10 AMP
Matthew 5:48 New King James Version
Mark 9:23 New King James Version
Romans 12:2 NKJV
Romans 12:17 NKJV
Ephesians 4:22, 23 AMP
Philippians 4:13 NKJV

Books and Reference Material

Alfred Adler "The Art of Loving"

Nathaniel Braden "The Psychology of Self-Esteem"

Annotated Guides "Great Artist" by Robert Cummings

The World Almanac 2007

Chris Hayes "Suits On Game On"

Christopher's Dictionary

(Webster can have one, why cant I?)

Infit: Your inside attire such as; emotions, hopes, dreams, goals, confidence, self-esteem, aspirations, self-image.

Physical Real Estate: Any outer attribute such as; muscles, breasts, rear end, facial features, hair and physique.

Outfit: Your outer clothing anything you put on.

What the Hockey puck: what the heck!

Masterpiece: What God made that is you. Every part of your being!

Water Bottle: Your mental water full of positive affirmations about yourself.

Love: strong affection for another arising out of kinship or personal ties. (2) Caring about yourself and loving what God gave you in order to pass it on to others!.

Acknowledgements

*TO MY FRAT brother ΦΒΣ/ big brother ΦΒΣ/
spiritual advisor/ the man that kept me from walking
out the door on God, Chris "Peto" Hayes. Man I can
not put in to words how much I want to thank you
for intervening that hot summer day at Barnes and
Nobles! If it were not for you taking time out to tell me
about your book we would have never met. Sometimes
the things you need the most are right next to you!
You just have to ask God for the ability to realize it! I
love you and your family like we are related by blood!
Whoa I know what you are saying right now, "Man
we are related by the blood of Christ!" You always*

keep me on my toes when it comes to our Father! Thank you man and the best is yet to come for you! PUT ME IN THE GAME COACH!

To my editor and friend Wendi! With out you this book would not be as polished as it is! I am so happy I met you that one day in Calabasas! I told you God put you in my path in a divine way! I thank you for keeping me engaged in the writing of this book, and just when I thought I could not make the corrections you wanted me to, you flicked me in my ear and said you can do it! Thank you for all the encouragement and for working with me when I did not have the money to pay you! This is just the beginning! We have 11 more to go! Remember what you wrote on the books when I first gave them to you? 10,000,000 copies each!

I would like to thank my Business Manager Christine A. McDougall of KM Management, Inc and her daughter Kelsey for all the support that they have given me. I will never forget the first day we met on that hot summer day at the pool! Oh Thank you for my nick name ("Book")!

I would like to thank Nevelyn for reading my book when it was on notebook paper! Thank you for telling me I can do it and that I was getting ready to change lives!

I would like to thank Niki for helping me see where I left some people out! You know what I am talking about! May God bless you and your family always!

I would like to thank Trisha for making me read my book out loud to her! I didn't know what you were doing by making me read it out loud, but I get it now!

I would like to thank LaVont Guillory for sowing a seed in my project and giving me the opportunity to get my dream off the ground! Brother you are a blessing and God has bigger plans for you then you can imagine! Thank you for believing in me and my message! May God Bless You and everybody over there at The Beauty Market in So Cal!

I want to thank my big sister Donna for sowing a seed into my project thanks for looking out for your little bro! And my big brother Keith we are there! My other big brother DS hold it down you are always in my prayers!

I want to thank all my family and friends that made sure I made it this far to do what God planned *for me to do from birth! Nuri, The Trust Family, Dee Dee, Drew, Sean, Tina, Aunt Edna, Aunt Lisa, Uncle K, Deacon Buford, Pastor Stafford, Pastor Mel, Dr. Perri Johnson, Uncle John, Warren Jabali, The Armstrong Family, Sherri, My Palestine Family, My In His Presence Family, My ZBET Family, Drs. Nelson & Anne Johnson, My God Mothers; Ann, Pam, Hope, & Jamesetta. My Little Rock Family, Crowell Family, My first mentor and Pastor the late Rev. Earl Abel, Silvester, Renee, Angela, Jim & Webster my second family, James Edwards, The Hatten Family, Rhonda & Raymond Beaver, Pat Prescott, Jake, Sean Tyler, Dee Tha Barber, Lorenzo Ice Tea Thomas, Big Lip, Kurt Hudson, Delawn Leggett, Larry Henry, Lydia, Herico, T David, Dr. Laurel Johnson, Dewey Hughes, Dan Weiner, and Pauline! We are ok now! If I did not say your name I am sorry, send me an email and I will add it in the next book! I have 11 more to go! www.cbjpublishing. com*

I want to thank the staff over at Barnes and Noble Café in Calabasas! Thanks for the Tea!

Last but definitely not least I want to thank my ex-fiancé (you know who you are) and everybody else who did not believe in me! Because it is due to their inability to see my true value that allowed me to discover what I really was worth! To my readers it is people like this including your enemies that give us the motivation to do the best we can! Remember this scripture for people like that; "The Lord will cause your enemies who rise against you to be defeated before your face; they shall come out against you one way and flee before you seven ways (Deuteronomy 28:7).

About the Author

Christopher Johnson born in Kansas City, Missouri currently residing in Los Angeles, California, by way of Miami! He started his company Cee Jay's Fit 4 TV Kids in 2006 after deciding to step away from a 14year career in the *Radio Entertainment Industry,* where he is a personal trainer to Hollywood Celebrity Kids. A former *Teen Star Correspondent* for "*The Kansas City Star Newspaper.*" He also is a motivational/inspirational speaker, a former AAU Track Coach. He is also the creator of a non-for profit organization called "*Let Everybody Read*" that is spearheading the push to get more book stores like Barnes and Noble and Borders to set anchor in low income areas. To give people a choice to invest their monies in a future of knowledge! Christopher is not a doctor or a pastor but he is a real person without a title that can help anyone with a title!

I have a passionate, energetic message that has inspired millions of people that I have come in contact with throughout my life.

Christopher is a new up and coming future *New York Times Best Selling Author!* With 10 books to his credit in the publishing process, *"Getting Dressed From The Inside"* is just the first taste. This book as well as *"Confidence, Where Does It Come From, and How Do I Get IT", Hello, My Name Is; Not My Body", " When God Talks To You After Hours", Self Esteem Is All That Matters", Confidences Of A BLACK MAN",* and *The 10 steps To The Gorgeous & Beautiful You",* are all going to help individuals like yourself change their image and help them to get away from the *stereo-type style* of how we view ourselves.

Printed in the United States
99562LV00001B

9 781434 353993